Bygone Truro

EXALTATUM CORNU IN DEO

'The ancient arms and common seales of the towne and borroughe of Trwro'.
Truro became Cornwall's only city in 1877. When its much prized city status was
threatened with local government re-organisation in 1974, a deputation of proud
and indignant Truronians went to Westminster to put forward their case—and won.
And so, on 1 April 1974, Her Majesty Queen Elizabeth II was pleased to re-confer
the city's status with Letters Patent.
(Coat of arms reproduced by courtesy of Truro City Council)

BYGONE TRURO

Sheila Bird

Phillimore

1986

Published by
PHILLIMORE & CO. LTD.,
Shopwyke Hall, Chichester, Sussex, England

ISBN 0 85033 609 0

Printed and bound in Great Britain by
BIDDLES LTD.
Guildford, Surrey

To all my friends
around Truro and the river

LIST OF ILLUSTRATIONS

ACKNOWLEDGEMENTS

The author and publisher would like to thank
The Royal Institution of Cornwall, Truro,
for the extensive use of their fine collection of photographs.

In compiling *Bygone Truro*, I have been greatly helped by many Truronians and the folk of the waterways who willingly allowed me to interview them. In particular I should like to acknowledge John Cockle, Jimmy Morrison, Peter Newman, Henry Merifield, Edward Merrifield, Frank Cock, Donald Gunn, William Gunn, Gerald Gunn, Randolph Gunn, Bill Kent, Reginald King, Tony Warren and Terry Heard. My thanks also go to Peter Gilson and the Royal Cornwall Polytechnic Society, Falmouth, Maurice Osborne, Fisher Barham, Terry Barham and Gloria Parker for all their goodwill and co-operation in the use of their photographs and to Brian Errington and Arthur Moulding for high quality photographic work. Again, my thanks go to the Local Studies Department, Redruth Library, and The Royal Institution of Cornwall, Truro, and particularly to Terry Knight and Roger Penhallurick for all their help and interest and Mr. H. L. Douch for checking my work. I have also drawn on the archives of *The West Briton* and *The Royal Cornwall Gazette & Cornwall County News*, with their extremely high standards of journalism and reporting.

For the use of photographs I am indebted to The Royal Institution of Cornwall for numbers 1, 2, 3, 4, 5, 6, 7, 8, 12, 18, 26, 31, 33, 34, 35, 41, 42, 43, 44, 52, 53, 54, 55, 57, 58, 61, 63, 66, 67, 68, 69, 70, 73, 77, 98, 100, 101, 102, 107, 109, 110, 116, 117, 118, 119, 120, 121, 122, 123, 125, 127, 129, 130, 137, 138, 139, 140, 142, 143, 147; The Royal Cornwall Polytechnic Society, Falmouth, for numbers 9, 10, 27, 60, 64, 71, 83, 84, 85, 86, 87, 90, 95, 99, 128, 131, 132, 133, 134, 135, 136, 146, 152; John Cockle for numbers 30, 49, 51, 82, 94, 148, 149, 151; Fisher Barham for numbers 23, 28, 29, 59, 65, 141; Maurice Osborne for numbers 45, 46, 50, 91, 111; Jimmy Morrison for numbers 36, 37, 38, 39; William Gunn for numbers 17, 103, 144, 150; Mervyn Habgood for numbers 74, 81, 114; Roy Stribley for number 104 and Norman and Jim Benney for number 145. Numbers 11, 13, 14, 15, 16, 19, 20, 21, 22, 24, 25, 32, 47, 48, 56, 62, 72, 75, 76, 78, 79, 80, 88, 89, 92, 93, 105, 106, 108, 112, 113, 115, 124, 126 are from the author's own collection and numbers 40, 96 and 97 were taken by the author.

INTRODUCTION

History

Truro, situated at the head of a navigable creek where early roads converged, was a market town and prosperous port when Falmouth was just a tiny fishing settlement on the western shores of the estuary; in fact, as every Truronian knows:

> Truro was a thriving town
> When Falmouth was a furzy down.

As the natural centre of a large mining and agricultural area with easy maritime access through Falmouth Haven, it was able to exploit its early industrial and trading potential by water; its situation at the head of a creek rendered it less vulnerable to seaward attack.

The original settlement was around the castle of the Earls of Cornwall, on the steeply sloping ground between the rivers Kenwyn and Allen. The name 'Truro', derived from 'Tri-veru', signified a settlement on three rivers, the rivers in question being the Kenwyn, Allen and a stream, now difficult to find, which flows beneath the dual carriageway in Tregolls Road to join the estuary through a culvert near Boscawen Bridge.

Truro is thought to have been incorporated as a borough in the first half of the 12th century. It had a merchants' guild and was established by the king as one of the Duchy's four original 'stannary' towns, for the official testing and stamping of locally mined tin, and had the privilege of sending two members to the 'Model Parliament' of 1295. However, Truro's prosperity suffered severe setbacks as a result of the Black Death in 1349, and in consequence was granted a remission of taxes. The situation had improved by Tudor times, and Queen Elizabeth confirmed an earlier right of collecting dues on all goods loaded and unloaded throughout the entire length of the river, and in 1589 she granted a charter incorporating a mayor, four aldermen and 20 capital burgesses.

Largely as a result of its geographical situation, Truro has found itself caught up in various social, religious and political events. During the Civil War, in common with most of the county, it supported the Royalist cause, but found itself in an untenable situation in the face of Fairfax's advancing troops. The town surrendered to the Parliamentarians on Tresillian Bridge in 1646. When Charles II was restored to the throne, Falmouth, which had been a staunchly Royalist stronghold, was granted its charter by the king in 1661, thereby gaining river rights previously enjoyed by Truro. This grant was hotly disputed by the Truronians, and led to a court case which Truro lost. A demarcation line was established between Messack Point, St Just, and Tarra

Point, Mylor, and since that time it has been customary for Truro to re-establish its river rights in the ancient ceremony of 'beating the bounds'.

The decision of the Killigrews to press ahead with developing Falmouth as a port led to the decline of Truro and Penryn. Truro, which was becoming silted up and unable to accommodate the larger ocean going vessels, began to concentrate principally on coastal and river trade. Miss Celia Fiennes, who visited Truro in 1695, described it as 'a ruinated, disregarded place'. But Truro's fate and fortunes improved in the 18th and 19th centuries when the price of metal rose, and traders and financiers moved in to capitalise on the wealth being generated by the mining industry. Thus Truro developed as the county's business and administrative centre as we know it today. Truronians have never understood why Bodmin is recognised as the official county town.

Daily life

The Elizabethan charter had granted the town a weekly market on Saturdays and occasional Wednesdays, and country folk enjoyed their trips to town, selling produce, and meeting their friends. The market became an occasion for eating, drinking and merrymaking. Traditionally, a glove was hung out at High Cross to mark the opening of the November Fair. Truro Whitsun Fair, which was an open event held on The Green, offered every kind of attraction and diversion to amaze and delight audiences, and earlier this century such companies as Sangers, Bostocks, Robert Fossetts, Chapmans, Barrys, Bertram Mills and John Swallows all brought their circuses to town.

In former times Truronians went awassailing through the streets over Christmas and the New Year, during the course of which cider was drunk from gaily decorated bowls, and money collected for the needy. Although in Old English 'wassail' means 'to be of good cheer', this ceremony was also designed to ward off evil spirits. Perhaps with this end in mind there was another local custom of 'singing funerals' when there would be rousing, processional hymn singing accompanied by brass bands.

Possessing a Dominican Friary in the 13th century, Truro had long played a significant part in the religious life of the county. It had a large number of churches of all denominations; a situation which caused a Falmouthian to remark, 'Truro – 'tis all clocks and bells'! John Wesley, whose famous sermons preached in the open air reached their peak at Gwennap Pit in the mid-18th century, when multitudes of seemingly Biblical proportions flocked to hear him, also preached at various churches in Truro. Cornish folk were attracted by his direct approach and compelling style. Life revolved around the church or chapel, for it was the place where people could meet and get to know each other. Everyone knew what everyone else was doing; a situation which helped to keep many a potential young tearaway on the straight and narrow.

Cleanliness is supposedly next to godliness, but in the days before the links between hygiene and health were fully appreciated, dung heaps were often deposited in the streets. The area near the polluted waterways was particularly offensive, and even in comparatively recent times rats and dogs scavenged around the quaysides and warehouses. With open-drains frequently contaminating water supplies, it is not surprising that townsfolk fell victim to cholera, smallpox and other horrifying diseases. Eminent Truronians remained aloof from such squalor, and, reflecting this attitude, the prison, almshouses and workhouse were sited close together, creating a neat package of Truro's social problems comfortably distanced from respectable folk. Men and women could be apprehended for trifling offences, and punishments were harsh.

The inmates of the workhouse were clothed, housed and employed by the parish, but the funds were grudgingly administered, for it was felt that every encouragement to make the poor find themselves employment should be given. This philosophy was successful inasmuch as the prospect of ending up in the workhouse was a tremendous incentive for keeping out of it.

During the 18th century, when hungry miners angrily marched on Truro, the militia was brought in to handle the situation, and when mining was in decline thousands of Cornish miners left these shores for a brighter future in Australia, New Zealand, Nova Scotia or America.

Until the 1830s parish watchmen had been responsible for law and order, but in 1838 the town council appointed a full-time inspector and five constables, and issued them with smart uniforms, staffs, rattles and handcuffs. By 1905 there was a borough police station and gaol attached to the Town Hall and Market House in Boscawen Street. The town, with its winding 'opes' and cramped buildings, had always been at risk from fire, and in 1728 a water engine equipped with leather buckets was in use. In 1868 a voluntary fire brigade was set up, financed by insurance companies and public donations, and the arrival of new fire engines was always a cause for great jubilation.

Ordinary folk who worked hard, also played hard, and knew how to celebrate. In the earlier part of this century when few could afford the luxury of holidays, Whit Monday and August Bank Holiday Monday were anticipated with relish, and savoured in retrospect. Some went for rail excursions, while horse-drawn carts and waggonettes were sometimes chartered by firms as a treat for their employees. River trips were particularly popular, and many regattas were held around the area. On Easter Monday, the young manhood flexed its collective muscles as rowing, football and rugby teams vied for supremacy, encouraged by large and appreciative crowds. Other recreations included roller skating, cycling, archery, gymnastics, cricket and sailing.

Until the Reformation, the provision of education had been the responsibility of the church, but in the 16th century, the monasteries having been dissolved and the desirability of education being recognised, the merchant classes began to found schools. When Truro Grammar School was founded in 1549, it was the only grammar school in Cornwall, and Truro has long been proud of its fine schools with the many former scholars they have sent forth to make their way in the world.

Truro had enjoyed early recognition as a cultural centre. In 1818 Cornwall Literary and Philosophical Society was established with the objective of furthering the sciences and the humanities. It later became known as the Royal Institution of Cornwall after George IV gave it his patronage. Its River Street premises were opened by the Prince of Wales in 1919. Towards the end of the 19th century literary and Bible classes were held around the town, and there were opportunities to participate in art and music. Lectures and concerts were held in the Public Rooms, which Tennyson visited on one occasion. Prior to the First World War, the thinking folk of Truro also flocked to the Gilchrist lectures, held bi-annually.

Fashionable folk who had stylish town houses in Truro attended theatrical performances at the Town Hall and, to cater for these cultural tastes, a theatre was built at High Cross in 1787. The Rev. Richard Warner described it as a 'gay and elegant town', for the season was one hectic whirl of theatre-going, parties and balls, and exhausting sessions at the card tables; a lifestyle spiced still further when dashing young officers were quartered around the town.

Today, the dignified cathedral with its handsome spires seems so much a part of Truro's essential character that it is difficult to realise that it is comparatively new, having been built only about 100 years ago. In August 1877, the *London Gazette* announced: 'The Queen has been pleased by Letters Patent under the Great Seal of the United Kingdom, bearing the date 28th day of August 1877, to ordain and declare that the borough of Truro, in the County of Cornwall shall be a city, and shall be called and styled "the City of Truro in the county of Cornwall"'. Much controversy surrounded the hemmed-in choice of site, which, it was argued, allowed no quiet close, nor any opportunity to view the building to advantage. However, the new cathedral, the first to have been built in England for 800 years, was a triumph. It cleverly incorporates part of the old parish church and reflects the Early English Gothic style. The foundation stones were laid on 20 May 1880, and the building took 30 years to complete. Dr. Edward White Benson, the first Bishop of Truro, was installed in the old vicarage house at Kenwyn, built in 1780 and re-named 'Lis Escop' (Bishop's Court). John Wesley, who stayed there in 1785, described it as 'a house fit for a nobleman, and the most beautifully situated of any I have seen in the county'.

In addition to a religious, educational and cultural heritage, the town developed a tradition of medical care with the setting up of the Royal Cornwall Infirmary in the late 18th century, and the Truro Dispensary in the mid-19th century; both provided free treatment for the poor. Since those early times, Truro has established a fine tradition of caring for the sick.

Communications: land and sea

Truro was on the early waggon routes into Cornwall, and stagecoaches plied between Torpoint and Truro in the 18th century. Following the completion of the new turnpike road from Tresillian more than a century ago, the spectacle of fast, gleaming mailcoaches with red-coated, plume-hatted guards sounding their brass horns on their downward approach to town must have been exciting. Although the routes into town were reasonably good, its thoroughfares produced dustclouds in summer and quagmires in winter. The streets of Truro were busy with horse buses and horse vans, which formed regular communication links with the surrounding towns and villages.

There were also reliable ferry connections with Falmouth and other waterside places, and the arrival of the railway in 1859 further improved communications. In the days before the widespread use of the motor car, when rail travel was very popular, Truro station was a scene of much activity and formed the background for many emotional departures in times of war. In February 1900, Truronians cheered enthusiastically as 11 of their number departed for service in the South African Boer War, and on their return patriotically-bedecked Boscawen Street played its customary centre stage role as processions, bands and exuberant revellers passed through, and church bells pealed in exultation.

Truro still maintained its maritime links until the Second World War, and the distinctive shallow draught Truro river barges, capable of penetrating the silting-up creeks, were evolved. River barges such as the *Sunbeam, Swift, Greyhound* and *Maggie*, which carried about 40 tons, with open holds, and decked fore and aft, traded up and down the Fal and Truro rivers, round to Gweek and to Tresillian and up the Ruan river. Bigger vessels, capable of carrying 50 to 80 tons, such as the *Silex, Dorothy, Emma, J & R* and *Sweet May*, known as 'smacks' or 'outside' barges, operated around the river and Falmouth, round to Plymouth and down to Porthoustock on the Lizard coast where they picked up quarried roadstone. Ketches, which were larger vessels, traded with Liverpool and the Irish coast and round to the Humber. Bigger vessels unable to get upstream as far as Truro unloaded at Falmouth or off Malpas, and their cargoes were transported upstream by barge. Vessels which lay in Malpas Reach with imported timber for Harvey's would be discharged onto barges, and sometimes secured timber rafts were floated upstream to the timber ponds at Truro, where they were left to season.

Old mariners recall the happy days aboard the sailing barges, ketches and barquentines, although life beneath the billowing canvas, when the hours were long and the going could be tough, was not always easy. Truro river barges, converging at points downstream, would hoist every inch of sail on reaching Black Rock, in readiness for the exhilarating race to Porthoustock. Bows thrust through the creaming, silvery waters and friendly dolphins escorted the spectacular flotilla down the Lizard coast. In those days when seafarers were expected to turn their hand to anything that needed doing, it was not merely a job, but a way of life as members of a special fraternity, with a subtle blend of comradeship and rivalry.

Mr. Chellew of Feock, whose offices were in Boscawen Street, owned a fleet of freighters with names prefixed by 'pen'. They included *Penover, Penmount, Penverne, Penhallow, Penhale* and *Pengreep*, and they worked out of Cardiff. Mr. Hitchens of Feock was mate aboard the *Pengreep* and at the outbreak of the First World War Mr. Henry Merifield, also of Feock served aboard that ship.

Deep-rooted in tradition, old rivalries die hard, for there has long been competition between Falmouthians and Truronians, and the folk of the upper creeks; a state of affairs which sometimes manifests itself around the oyster beds. Oyster dredging has been a way of life in these parts since the time of the Romans and possibly even earlier, and methods can have changed very little. From the early part of this century permits had to be obtained from the river authorities in Truro, and the fishermen were required to pay a certain amount for each dredge. Dredges, resembling netted bags, held open by a rigid framework, were dragged slowly along the riverbed, hauled aboard and the catch sorted. Smaller oysters were returned to the water to allow them to mature, while water bailiffs patrolled the area to ensure that regulations were not infringed.

Prior to the Second World War, a form of fishing known as 'hacking' was popular in the upper creeks when mullet used to head upstream in large shoals, leaving tell-tale ripples on the surface of the water like bubbles from a boiling kettle. At this signal, the fishermen of Malpas, Coombe, St Clement and all the places around the creeks would rush for their boats, and string long, weighted nets across the river. At the turn of the tide the fish would be trapped, and after the fishermen had taken what they wanted, local folk were free to venture out into the mud channels to collect dabs, flounder and other fish which were there for the gathering. Before the last war mullet, dabs, pollack and bream were plentiful around Truro and Falmouth, but the area was over-fished, and today these and many other types of fish are rare.

There has long been a tradition of ships being laid up in the river, with dues payable to the Truro authorities. In the last century there were reports of large numbers of ships being laid up in the river, having become 'warbound', or awaiting orders. There is a clear 50-foot level of water at low tide off Tolverne, with an 18-foot rise and fall, making this a particularly suitable area for big ships in times of recession. This reached a peak between the two wars, and again more recently as demand called for a move from conventional ships to container ships; now in the 1980s, other ships await an economic upturn.

Truro at war

At the outbreak of war in 1914, the Bishop of Truro urged his flock to 'Pray devoutly, hammer away stoutly ...'. As young men responded to their call of patriotic duty and local craft were taken over for wartime service, 381 American passengers aboard the German cruise liners *Kronprincessen Cecilie* and *Prinz Adalbert*, who had been anticipating the cruise of a lifetime, experienced just that. They were taken ashore at Falmouth by local boatmen, while men of the 4th Battalion of the Duke of Cornwall's Light Infantry and others, together with all the horses that could be commandeered, were placed aboard the ship in readiness for war. The German seamen, who suddenly found themselves prisoners at the outbreak of war were temporarily held in the old Truro workhouse, known as the 'Union'. Older Truronians recall the sight of Catholic prisoners being marched through the streets to attend Mass at the church. Dutch merchant ships, distinctively painted overall to signify their neutrality, and expecting the international rules of war to be observed, fell victim to German submarines and desperately sought refuge up the river.

While the men were away at war, women took over essential work on the land and in factories, as well as joining the auxiliary services and taking part in fund-raising activities. Truro became a reception centre for wounded servicemen. When resources were overstretched, a temporary naval hospital was opened at St Clement in 1915 and remained in use until the end of the war. There were food shortages; those families unable to grow their own produce would walk out along the Old Falmouth Road, to meet Mr. Burnett, who travelled up from Porth Kea to sell his produce to Truro households from his two-wheeled, horse-drawn cart.

The streets of the city were bedecked for the 'Peace Day Parade', to mark the end of the conflict. Solid-tyred lorries converged on The Green, where an old field gun was sited for many years, and people assembled for the parade of returned troops, with the Union flag proudly held aloft.

Between the two world wars, secret work was carried out on anti-submarine devices and an underground system of oil pipelines at Falmouth. The river, with its oil store at Malpas, was a highly sensitive area, and its course was used as a navigational 'fix' by German planes in daylight hours to plot night-time bombing targets. Pleasure craft including *Princess Victoria* and *Queen of the Fal* were commandeered to act as patrol vessels and tender ships, while ships laid up in the Fal, including *Dunera* and *Fairlea*, were brought out of retirement to serve as troopships, and a Truro Home Guard River Patrol was hurriedly set up.

In common with the rest of Britain, the citizens of Truro were given instructions to carry gas masks at all times, to black out their houses, build air raid shelters, grow their own food, 'make do and mend', collect salvage and save money for the war effort. Although Falmouth had taken an early battering, life at the beginning of the war tended to go on much as before in Truro. There was controversy about the provision for public air raid shelters, and about the safety of children caught in an air raid on their way to and from school. Signposts around the area were removed. Auxiliary nurses responded to the Ministry of Health's appeal to them to register, and branches of the W.R.V.S., A.R.P., Home Guard and National Fire Service were formed. Static water tanks were installed around the city, which was divided into 20 sections with men appointed as fire watchers and fire beaters in each section.

The River Patrol was particularly active at night, checking along the shores and wooded banks for German parachutists. They were issued with Naval-type battledress and rifles. No one was allowed on the river after dark for reasons of security, much to the regret of local fishermen whose best fishing was at that time. Canvas decoy vessels, lit up at night, were used on the river to confuse the enemy. But despite all this, everyday life in Truro had an air of normality, a situation encouraged by the authorities, for it was government policy to keep morale high in wartime Britain. In 1940 the Kent and England Test cricketer Frank Woolley took part in a schools match at Treyew Road; the summer sales went ahead as usual, with some folk stocking up with rationed goods – just in case; and the Truro City Band, with a 'scratch' team replacing musicians away on active service, played in Boscawen Park for a B.B.C. broadcast. Activities such as this were designed to 'inspire and please a nation that has a grim task to perform ... Let the people sing, let the people dance, and let the people listen to the band'. In fact the cinema, Sunday concerts and the work of the Royal Institution of Cornwall continued more or less unhindered throughout the duration of the war.

Some Truro households felt the burden of war more through the behaviour of unruly London evacuees beneath their roofs, than from the enemy without, and there was much comment in the local papers of the time which advocated that scruffy, unruly children could be tamed in decent, clean homes with firm, kindly discipline; with love and understanding, rather than the more popular philosophy that rude, dirty children should be matched to the sort of places where they might feel more at home. While some Truronians were finding it difficult to adjust themselves to the evacuees in their midst, those families in turn were finding it difficult to adjust to the Cornish way of life, and yearned for the familiar streets of London. When there was an apparent lull in the action, around December 1940, homesick Londoners started drifting back to the city, much to the consternation of caring local people. There was a general false sense of security, and the newspapers, reminding them that 'careless talk costs lives', pointed out 'Nobody is being left out of this war ... The people to be respected here in Truro are the silent ones and not those garrulous folk flushed with pleasure at being able to hold a group spellbound by relating that so and so has heard that parachutists have landed, or that defences are being erected in such and such a location. The game we are now about is one of life and death'.

Local people did well in producing home-grown food; Women's Institutes acquired canning machines and Truronians were encouraged to keep bees. A 'British Restaurant' was set up to free harassed mothers and evacuee hostesses to serve their country in the auxiliary services, as land girls, munitions workers or fund raisers. In

1940 the Bishop of Truro urged his flock to share their Christmas firesides with servicemen and women far away from their own. Servicemen overseas were sent mementoes to show that they were not forgotten. There was a surge of enthusiasm for fund raising events, which engendered competition amongst local towns and villages, with *War Weapons Week*, *Warship Week*, *Wings For Victory Week*, *Salute The Soldier Week*, and culminating with *Thanksgiving Week*. Truronians, well practised in staging such occasions, organised stirring parades of the defence services through the streets, with sports, competitions, music and dancing.

The villagers of Malpas had worked hard to create fine communal shelters, but they were taken completely by surprise on the night of Easter Monday 1941, when without any warning there was a terrific explosion, and for a moment it seemed as if the whole of Malpas had been blown up. However, the victim was an old French destroyer anchored off Tolverne, which was blasted into three parts by a bomb. Mrs. Rodney Newman of Tolverne later received a letter of thanks from His Majesty's Naval Base at Falmouth for looking after the two bombed shipkeepers. Malpas experienced its first – and last – raid after the 'red' warning had sounded and enemy planes approached with the apparent intention of bombing the oil depot; but the tide was out, and the bombs landed in the nearby mud, merely spattering the depot and killing only an unlucky duck.

For one brief period of the war, the rural area of Truro was statistically the most bombed in the country. On 6 August 1942, Truronians were taken by surprise when German planes came in over the river and bombed the Royal Infirmary, killing a number of patients and staff. The blast shook the nearby *Plaza* cinema, and terrified filmgoers rushed for the exits as the screen appeared to come towards them. The rescue services and volunteers worked into the night at the hospital, clearing the rubble and pulling out the injured and dead.

As the war progressed, Truro witnessed local activities building up for the invasion of Normandy. From 1943-44, an assortment of 'Yanks' was billeted in the area; officers took over some of the bigger buildings, while tents appeared on the hillsides and Nissen huts were constructed in wooded areas. Boscawen Park became the focus of activity where hundreds of landing craft were assembled; concrete roads and slipways were built for the embarkation of troops at Tolverne, Turnaware, Mylor and Falmouth. Tolverne cottage was taken over by American 'Top Brass', and 13 separate telephone lines were installed in the office, which is now a bar. Equipment was hidden amongst the trees, ack-ack guns were emplaced in the woods and sentries guarded the area. In 1943, the River Patrol was leaving nothing to chance, for boatman Rodney Newman of Tolverne Cottage was out on the river as usual, when two warning shots were fired over his head and he was challenged. The patrol then escorted him home and scrutinised his official documents. 1943 marked the Truro Home Guard's third birthday, which was celebrated in the heart of the city with parades and demonstrations of their training and weaponry. Following the D-Day departure for France in 1944, Canon R. H. Roberts, Senior Chaplain to the forces, paid tribute to their work during a service in the cathedral.

On 9 May 1945 *The Royal Cornwall Gazette & Cornwall County News* carried a headline: 'GERMANY GIVES IN UNCONDITIONALLY'. The Prime Minister's broadcast was relayed in Boscawen Street, there was a service of thanksgiving in the cathedral, then Truronians, all poised for traditional boisterous jollification, let their hair down with a grand finale of parades, followed by music and dancing through the floodlit streets.

BIBLIOGRAPHY

Barham, Fisher, *The Creation of a Cathedral*, 1976.
Barrett, Rex, *Memories of a Truronian in War and Peace*.
Barrett, Rex, *Life in Edwardian Truro*, 1977.
Barrett, Rex, *Stately Homes in and around Truro*.
Burley, W. J., *City of Truro 1877 - 1977*, 1977.
Davidson, R. E., *The History of Truro Grammar and Cathedral School*.
Douch, H. L., *The Book of Truro*, 1977.
Farr, Grahame, *West Country Passenger Steamers*, 1956.
Hamilton Jenkins, A. K., *Cornwall and its People*, 1970.
Murray, John, *A Handbook for Travellers in Devon and Cornwall*, 1865.
Osborn, J. Lee, *Homeland Handbook: Falmouth, Truro and the River Fal*.
Noall, Cyril, *Harveys 200 years of Trading*, 1979.
Ward, C. S. and Baddeley, M. J. B., *Thorough Guide: South Devon and South Cornwall*, 1895.

Newspapers

The Graphic
The Illustrated London News
Royal Cornwall County Gazette
The West Briton

The Plates

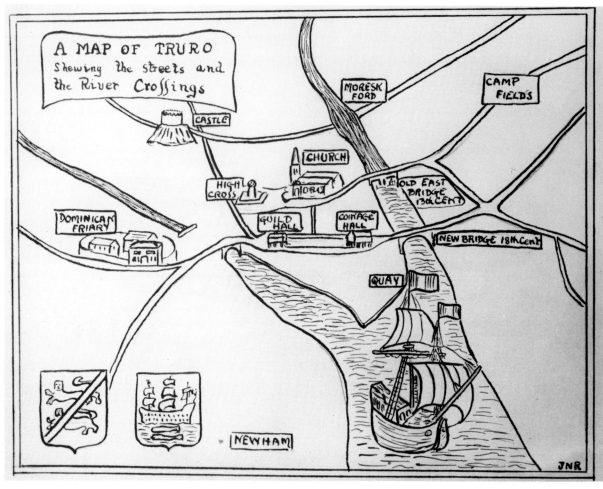

1. This sketchmap by John Rosewarne, one-time president of the Royal Institution of Cornwall, shows early routes into the town.

2. This reconstruction shows how the town may have looked in the 13th century, well-placed to exploit its position at the head of a branching estuarine inlet.

Early Days

3.   Truro from Kenwyn churchyard: an engraving by W. Varley, 1806.

4. *(opposite above)* As the port became silted up, it was no longer able to accommodate ocean-going vessels, and concentrated on coastal and river trade. This engraving shows Truro in 1816, viewed from Poltisco.

5. *(opposite below)* The Guildhall and other buildings in Middle Row, in the centre of what is now Boscawen Street, were demolished to make room for traffic. Middle Row is seen here as it appeared about 1810 in a reconstruction by Rex Carter.

6. *(above)* The medieval Coinage Hall, which also served for some time as the Court of the Vice Warden of the Stannaries, stood on a site later occupied by the Trustee Savings Bank.

7. *(below left)* The obverse side of a Charles I half-crown, minted in Truro. The town had by that time long been one of the four stannary towns of Cornwall, officially permitted to test and approve the quality of tin.

8. *(below right)* The reverse side of a Charles I half-crown.

Evolution of a City

9. This photograph, taken from Poltisco about 1876, shows Brunel's wooden-topped viaduct straddling the two valleys, smoke from the smelting works at Carvedras (background, centre left) and the old parish church of St Mary's, on the site now occupied by the cathedral.

10. In this photograph, taken about 1900, the main body of the cathedral has been completed, but work is still being carried out on the towers. Brunel's viaduct is still visible in the background. The section of river in front of the bridge was later covered over.

11. By 1915 the cathedral had gained its spire, and the old viaduct had been replaced by a stone and brick construction.

Streets and Buildings

12. *(above)* This is an idealised view of the area at the top of Lemon Street published by William Lake about 1840. Leafy and gracious, with stylish houses, scrubbed doorsteps and polished brasswork, this was where Truro's 'quality' lived.

13. *(opposite above)* The *Red Lion* hotel, Boscawen Street, *c.* 1890. This elegant building had to be demolished after being hit by a runaway lorry in the 1960s.

14. *(opposite below)* Looking westwards along Boscawen Street, towards City Bank, about 1900. The street was renamed in honour of Lord Falmouth's family, the Tregothnans. The horse trough was erected by the Metropolitan Horse Trough Drinking Association, a national body concerned with the welfare of horses.

Red Lion Hotel,
Truro

15. Looking eastwards along Boscawen Street, just after the First World War, when horse-drawn traffic was giving way to motorised vehicles. In the centre distance is the cabmen's shelter, provided by the National Cabmen's Shelter Association.

16. The Municipal Buildings, Boscawen Street, c. 1900. On 11 November 1914 a fire broke out destroying most of the interior of the City Hall, and causing the blazing clocktower to crash through the roof. A replacement clock was presented by an anonymous donor.

17. Looking towards Ferris Town beneath Brunel's trestle-topped viaduct, St George's Road, around 1880. An old guidebook states that 'those timber viaducts ... severely tried the nerves of passengers in the 19th century; but there was never an accident with one of them, though they extended along the line from Ivybridge in Devon'.

18. The wooden viaduct was supported by pillars of stone, and although it was replaced by a new construction in 1902, as we see here, the original pillars remain alongside their replacements.

19.   From almost the same vantage point as in no. 17, two gentlemen pause to admire the newly-completed replacement viaduct in 1904.

20.   Children enjoyed playing in Waterfall Gardens, adjacent to St George's Chapel, seen here around the turn of the century. The park closed at dusk when park keeper Mr. Treweek rang a bell and shouted 'All out! All out!'

21. The Victoria Gardens were opened in 1898. The bandstand, capped with a weather vane, is still a favourite venue for brass bands from all over Cornwall.

22. Quay Street, 1910. The old Mansion House is centre right; it was built in 1709 by Samuel Enys, who also developed Enys Quay. Having amassed a fortune from mining, the family had been property-owners in Truro from the 15th century.

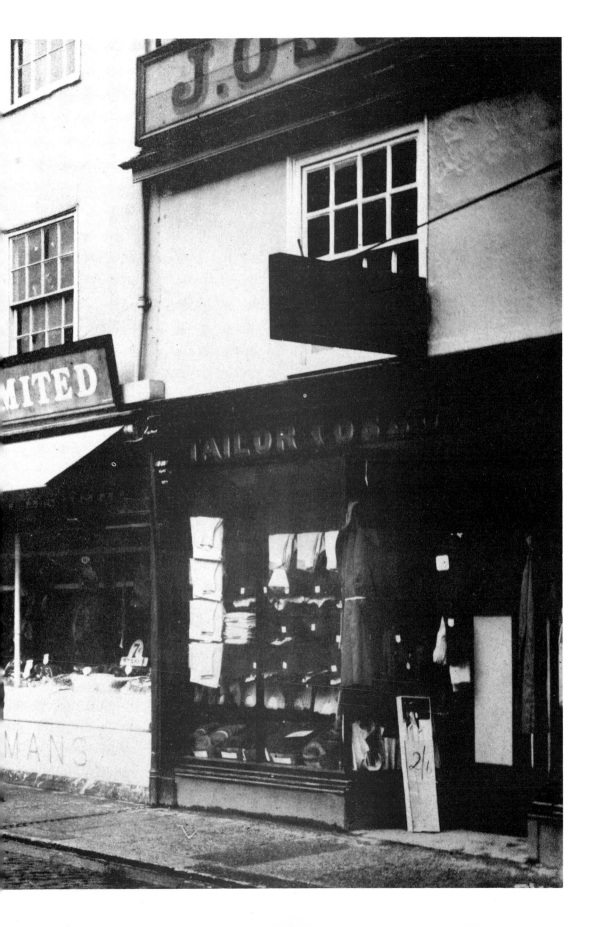

Truro. Victoria Place.

Truro
Lander Column

23. *(overleaf)* King Street, *c.* 1910. Many shopowners lived over their premises, and sometimes also had workshops at the back, as in the case of tailors and bootmakers.

24. *(above)* Victoria Place, about 1915. Like Boscawen Street and High Cross, this was a particularly busy area on market days.

25. *(left)* The Lander Statue honours the 'enterprise and sufferings of the brothers Richard and John Lander', African explorers. The memorial is seen here about 1910.

26. This photograph of the River Allen between St Clement's Bridge and New Bridge, *c*. 1930, gives a romantic glimpse of bygone Truro. However, waterside stores and warehouses attracted rats, and dogs roamed the streets scavenging for debris. The waters were polluted, and around the waterways it was particularly smelly.

27. A child going to school past the Lemon Street archway which originally led to livery stables.

28. The river was the lifeblood of Truro. Here we see the navigable stretch extending to the bottom of Lemon Street, with the market house (centre, right) backing onto the quay. Within living memory, it was not uncommon to see as many as six schooners alongside this quay.

Port of Truro

29. *(overleaf)* River barges such as these, seen by Lemon Quay about 1905, were a familiar sight around the waterways until just after the Second World War. This section of the river was covered over in 1923.

30. *(above)* The schooner *Lizzie* and the ketch *Industry*, seen at Town Quay about 1890. *Lizzie*, which was owned by a consortium of Truro shareholders, has been recalled as a ship on which the crew worked hard, read the Bible and had empty bellies!

31. *(opposite above)* This photograph shows *Bessie* and two topsail schooners alongside Phoenix Wharf, formerly Trafalgar Wharf. Radio Cornwall now occupies the site of a former warehouse here.

32. *(opposite below)* The three-masted topsail schooner *Mary Barrow* was built by Leans of Falmouth for a Barrow shipowner, and she was originally registered in that town. Later, re-registered in Truro, she was to become the last ship to be Truro-owned. She had a fine figurehead and a chequered headboard. The *Mary Barrow* was wrecked off the Isle of Man about 1936.

33. *(above)* Reclamation plans to acquire more land around Lemon Quay had been drawn up since the mid-19th century, and in 1923 the river was covered over to create a car park.

34. *(opposite above)* Here we see the mayor and other leading Truronians performing the ancient ceremony of 'beating the bounds' at Messack Point on 1 August 1911.

35. *(opposite below)* Oyster dredging has taken place on the river since Roman times at least. This photograph dates from about 1905.

Trade by Water

36. *(opposite above)* Here Jimmy Morrison and Eddie Roberts are sailing back over the drift in Jimmy's boat *Mayflower*, off Messack Point, about to begin dredging for oysters.

37. *(opposite below)* Jimmy Morrison hauls the dredge aboard. On this occasion three dredges are being used, all of them over the port side.

38. *(above)* 'Tipping' the dredge.

39. *(right)* Here Jimmy Morrison is 'culling the dredge'. After being hauled out of the water the oysters are extricated from the nets and placed on the culling table to be sorted. Any less than two and five-eighths of an inch in diameter are returned to the water.

40. Gerald Gunn of Combe Creek demonstrates his shrimping net. Shrimping was carried out on low water spring tides between June and September. The shrimps were boiled and taken to Hayle to be sold.

41. A sailing barge discharging cargo at the tidal port of Tresillian, c. 1900. This once-flourishing little port is now completely silted up, a process accentuated by waste material from the mines being deposited upstream.

42. The timber ship *Rajore* (built in Southampton in 1882) off Maggoty Bank in 1903. Combe 'caffers', well-known for their capacity for hard work, came downstream to offload timber onto lighters, which were towed upstream to Harvey's timber yard. The silting-up port of Truro was no longer able to accommodate such large vessels.

43. In this sensitive photographic study of Harvey's timber ponds in 1903, the essence of mid-winter is conveyed.

44. *(above)* The timber yard: timber unloaded from Russian and Scandinavian ships anchored at Woodbury was sometimes chained together and rafted upstream where it would be left in timber ponds to season. Pitch pine was left to season for 12 months.

45. *(left)* A barquentine loading tin at Devoran, 1904. Devoran, on the shores of Restronguet Creek, was formerly a busy port linked to the mining areas by rail, supplying coal for the pumping machines and wood for pit props, and loading tin concentrates for smelting in South Wales. The creek is now silted up, but the remains of the old quaysides, wharves and railways are still visible.

46. In the heyday of waterborne trade, about 30-40 Truro river barges like *Mary*, seen here in the Perran river about 1910, traded around the waterways. They varied in capacity from 40 to 80 tons, and carried corn, tin, coal, roadstone, or any other cargo offered to them.

47. The pleasure steamer/tug *New Resolute*, built at Malpas in 1882, was skippered by Ernie Burley and crewed by his wife. The controls were notoriously unpredictable: 'full ahead' sometimes engaging 'full astern' and vice versa, with surprising consequences!

48. A river steamer passing Sunny Corner, *c.* 1910.

49. The two-masted schooner *Kate* was a familiar sight before the last war. She was the last sailing vessel brought into the harbour. She caught fire and sank at anchor off the Welsh coast in the mid-1930s.

50. Old mariners happily recall their youth aboard sailing barges such as the *Sweet May*, pictured here around 1920.

51. Ships laid up in the river about 1923. In the 1930s this practice reached epic proportions, with ships anchored five abreast from Woodbury to Turnaware Bar, and it reached another peak in the late 1960s and early 1970s.

Trade and Industry

52. *(above)* From 1710, Calenick was the site of smelting activity, and Mitchell and Company's large works is seen here about 1870.

53. *(opposite above)* Workers at Carvedras smelting works, photographed about 1893. This works, situated off St George's Road at the foot of Brunel's viaduct, was established before 1750. It later became the property of the Consolidated Tin Smelting Company Ltd., of Penzance. It ceased functioning in 1898.

54. *(opposite below)* Workmen at the site of the Carvedras works, about 1902. Brunel's viaduct is being replaced by brick and stone.

55. *(opposite above)* Oscar Blackford's printing works, *c.* 1890. Blackford's carried out lithographic and engraving work, published early postcards as well as the *Cornwall County News, Blackford's Railway Timetable*, and the *Truro Directory*, and were also commercial stationers. In 1919 they took over the *Royal Cornwall Gazette*, merging it with the *News*, and the latter was in turn taken over by the *West Briton* in 1951.

56. *(opposite below)* Webb & Company, *The Popular Drapers*, about 1905. Customers (who were *always* right) were greeted at the door and escorted to the appropriate smartly-dressed sales assistant.

57. *(right)* Advertisements like this, offering the hope of better prospects, attracted many Cornish folk to start a new life overseas. Towards the end of the 19th century, thousands of miners emigrated to America and Australia.

58. *(below)* Scawswater Mill on the River Allen was one of a series of mills used mostly for grinding corn and fulling cloth. By the end of the 19th century it was used as a steam sawmill by the Scawswater Saw Mills Company, run by Arthur Visick.

EMIGRATION
TO
SOUTH AUSTRALIA

Her Majesty's Colonization Commissioners having determined to dispatch in the course of a few weeks a large number of Emigrants, all eligible persons may obtain, by making an IMMEDIATE application, a

FREE PASSAGE!

The classes of persons now in requisition are
Agricultural Laborers,
SHEPHERDS, CARPENTERS
BLACKSMITHS
AND
STONE MASONS
And all Persons connected with Building.
Application to be made to
Mr. L LATIMER,
Rosewin-row, TRURO.

E. HEARD, PRINTER AND BOOKBINDER, BOSCAWEN-STREET, TRURO.

59. Here Martin's horse bus leaves the *Norway Inn* at Perranarworthal for Truro. Horse-buses, designed primarily to carry passengers, also carried some goods, and similarly horse-vans took a few passengers in the early days.

Transport and Services

60. *(overleaf)* The North Cornwall Coach departs from the *Red Lion* in Boscawen Street, watched by onlookers, about 1890.

61. *(above)* Fine folk with their carriages athwart the transom of the King Harry ferry *c.* 1880, arriving safely on the Feock shore to their waiting grooms and horses. This ferry passage linking the Roseland peninsula with the Truro district was important form the earliest times.

62. *(below)* This early chain ferry with its cabin and puffing steam may resemble a mechanised Noah's Ark, but it was nevertheless a great step forward when it was introduced at the end of the last century.

63. A busy scene at Malpas as the steamer *Princess Victoria* passes *Queen of the Fal*, and the ferryman takes up his oars just offshore. Across the water on the St Michael Penkevil side is the lovely 17th-century ferry cottage, with the former *Ship Inn* to the left. When strong winds funnel upstream, this passage becomes very treacherous — a '*mal pas*'.

64. The Malpas ferry was an important communication link with Truro, particularly on market days. A horse and waggon boat of the type seen here operated as recently as the 1930s, with delivery men crossing daily.

65. The Cornish Riviera Express.

66. The *Queen of the Fal*, seen here passing Trennick Row, was built by Cox and Company of Falmouth and registered in Truro. The River Fal Steamship Company operated summer cruises round the coast and up the 'Cornish Rhine'.

67. Truro railway station, *c.* 1910. The engine is the Bulldog class locomotive *Tasmania* (3457), which was built in January 1904, renumbered 3395 in 1912, and withdrawn in 1948.

68. R. and J. Lean's horse and furniture removal waggon outside Truro railway station around 1910. The driver had very little protection from the weather.

69. Criddle and Smith's fine Daimler delivery and removal van cut a dash locally just after the First World War. In addition to carrying out removal work, they were house agents, auctioneers and valuers, and later expanded into cabinet making, upholstery and decorating, and also had carpet warehouses. They were later taken over by Dingles of Plymouth.

70. Richard Thomas, the ice cream seller of Trennick Farm, Malpas, photographed on the football field at the back of Treyew Road c. 1930.

Truro's Rural Area

71. *(opposite above)* Carclew (*Cruc-lew*, meaning 'burial mound of Lew') was built in the Ionic style in 1728. It was appraoched by an impressive avenue of trees, and was one of Cornwall's grandest houses. It was at one time the home of William Lemon, after whom Lemon Street is named. Carclew was burnt down in 1934.

72. *(opposite below)* An idyllic rural scene at the village of Calenick around 1890, close to an area which was once industrial off the Old Falmouth Road, now quiet again. There was a candlemaking factory and ropeworks, and an ancient corn mill powered by the Nansavalon stream. The boatyard at the head of the creek produced vessels ranging from rowing boats to sailing barges.

73. *(above)* This delightful photograph, dating from 1890, captures the spirit of Ruan Lanihorne when the river was still navigable. Barges could still be manoeuvred at Sett Bridge until the last war.

74. *(below)* Tresillian Bridge, close to the gatehouse of Tregothnan, was the site of the surrender of the royalist general Sir Ralph Hopton to the parliamentarian Fairfax in 1646.

75. Tregothnan, built at 'the place of the twisting brook', was the seat of the powerful and influential Boscawen family. When it was completed in 1822, Lord Falmouth marked the occasion by presenting fat oxen to the parishioners of Kenwyn, Kea and Truro.

76. South-facing, and commanding magnificent views across the Fal estuary, Trelissick House was built in 1750. It was acquired in 1800 by Ralph Daniell, M.P. for Looe, who was reputedly the wealthiest man in Cornwall. The beautiful gardens are now administered by the National Trust and open to the public.

77. Until 1924 when a road was built Coombe Creek was accessible only by water, and the inhabitants had to be hard-working and self-sufficient. They sold their famous Kea plums in Truro and Falmouth, went oak-barking and oyster-dredging, and also unloaded timber ships. Here we see a 'Coombe Creeker' chopping logs.

78. The picturesque *Pandora Inn*, formerly the *Ship*, was renamed by Captain Edwards, whose vessel the *Pandora* was wrecked in the Pacific with great loss of life after he had captured the mutineers from Captain Bligh's ship the *Bounty*. Captain Edwards was dismissed from the Navy as a result and thus became a publican.

79. According to legend, King Henry VI once swam across the river with his horse at this point, hence the name 'King Harry Passage'. Truro river barges can be seen unloading by the ferry slopes on the Philleigh shore.

80. Malpas is situated where the Truro and Tresillian rivers converge. According to local Arthurian legends, it is here that Princess Iseult was ferried across the river from the Forest of Morrois (Moresk in St Clement) to King Mark's palace in Blanchland (Kea).

River Fal, Malpas.

81. Lord Falmouth's guests enjoyed river excursions, and dances held in the upper rooms of Tregothnan Boathouse. The ferrywoman Jenny Mopus transported guests to the boathouse and cooked potatoes in river water while she waited for them to emerge.

82. The attractive Pencalenick Estate gatehouse has long been a familiar landmark for travellers. Pencalenick, meaning 'end of the holly grove', once the property of actor Samuel Foote, was rebuilt in 1879 following a fire. Having been requisitioned by the army in the last war, it housed Italian prisoners before becoming the headquarters for U.S. troops in the area.

Religion

83. *(above)* St Mary's parish church, *c.* 1870. This church was partially incorporated into the new cathedral.

84. *(opposite above)* The cathedral was designed by Mr. J. L. Pearson, R.A.

85. *(opposite below)* Skilled stonemasons pause in their work in the 1880s. Granite from Mabe was used for the main exterior walls, and softer granite from St Stephen's for the interior. Mellow Bath stone was incorporated in the arches, columns and decorative dressings inside and out.

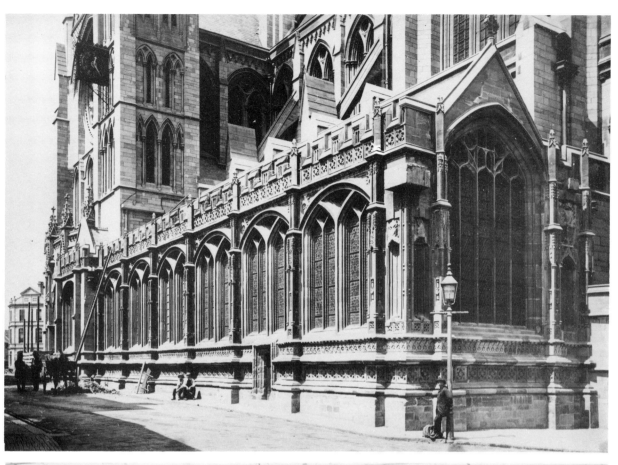

86. This photograph shows craftsmen at work on the west front, now a familiar sight fronting High Cross.

87. The west front and High Cross. High Cross was the terminus for the city's horse-buses which brought in shoppers from neighbouring towns and villages.

88. Easterly view of the completed cathedral, 1910.

89. Born at Twelveheads, Kea, 'Little' Billy Bray (1794-1868), who was also known as 'the miners' preacher', was a disciple of John Wesley and preached in a similarly compelling style. For over 40 years this 'most faithful servant of Christ' endeavoured to benefit the souls of fellow men.

BALDHU CHURCH
WHERE BILLY BRAY IS BURIED

BILLY BRAY

'THE KING'S SON'.

A NOTABLE
CORNISH MINER
AND PREACHER.

Born & Died
at
Twelve Heads
IN THE PARISH OF KEA
NEAR TRURO.

AGED 73 YEARS

MONUMENT ERECTED AT BALDHU
OVER THE GRAVE OF BILLY BRAY.
REGISTERED DESIGN 2515.

90. The west view of St Mary's, *c.* 1870. The dreaded sound of St Mary's bell signified death and disaster, particularly fires.

91. St Clement Churchtown, *c.* 1880. This was known as the 'church of Moresk' which was the ancient manor, seat of the earls of Cornwall. A slate-hung schoolroom was incorporated in the lychgate.

92.   Before fishermen put to sea, prayers were said in the church of Feock, whose ancient tower is seen here about 1890. The last sermon preached in the Cornish language was given here.

93.   Kenwyn church, commanding magnificent views of the river from its churchyard, was adjacent to the vicarage, which became the residence of the Bishop of Truro. This photograph was taken about 1904.

94. John Cockle, Senior, was a seafarer and ardent Salvationist who unfailingly attended 'Sally Army' functions when ashore. Former shipmates recalled him praying on his knees every night in the fo'castle.

95. Children greatly appreciated the annual Sunday School treats, particularly trips on the river to St Mawes or Falmouth. They usually took their own packed tea, which was supplemented by a large saffron bun and a drink.

Recollections of War

96. *(opposite above)* The Quaker meeting house at Come-to-Good was built in 1710, and the wooden loft was added seven years later.

97. *(opposite below)* Splendidly situated on St Just Creek, the 13th- to 15th-century church is set in a semi-tropical garden.

98. *(above)* A landgirl learns to milk with the aid of artificial udders.

99. Fund raising outside the *Daniell Arms*, 1914.

100. A stretcher case arrives at the County of Cornwall Royal Naval Auxiliary Hospital, and is transported from the ambulance to a ward.

101. While war meant suffering or death for many, for others, like these landgirls and farmworkers, it was literally a case of 'making hay' while the sun shone.

102. Christmas in Hain Ward, St Clement Hospital, 1917.

103. The war memorial, erected at the eastern end of Boscawen Street, adjacent to the sites of the former Coinage Hall and Town Hall.

104. The White Star liner *Laurentic*, seen here laid up in the King Harry Passage, went to war as an armed merchantman, and was sunk off the coast of Scotland. The three *Inver* tankers in the background were built in Belfast, and immediately laid up in the Fal having never carried a cargo. They saw wartime service as tankers and were all sunk.

105. Gas decontamination drill, 1940.

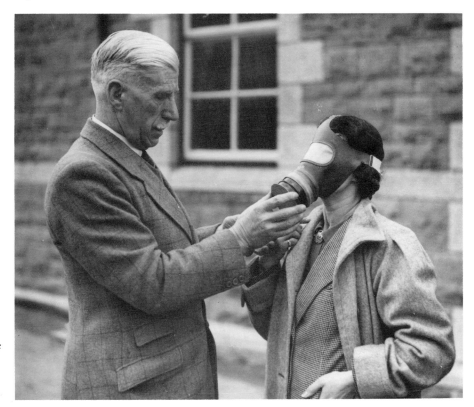

106. Major Gill instructs
in the correct fitting of the
gas mask, and tests its
effectiveness by holding
up a card which should be
drawn towards the mask.

107. Sandbagging around the Cathedral School, 1940.

108. During the war the National Fire Service was established to deal with the after-effects of bombing. A second fire station was opened in New Bridge Street, and in 1944 another new one was established in St George's Road.

109. Military vehicles outside HTP Motors (now the Creation Centre), 1941.

110. HTP Motors was taken over by the government for the construction and repair of aircraft components, particularly Spitfires. Later on guns and other equipment were produced in Truro and army vehicles repaired.

111. One section of the Home Guard, formed in the early days of the war, was Truro's River Patrol Home Guard. Their boats were fitted with Ross rifles, Lewis machine-guns and other anti-aircraft devices. They cruised the waterways looking for any suspicious characters.

112. Truro's Home Guard march along Boscawen Street.

113.   Members of the Red Cross march past the saluting base. The Truro branch was founded in 1910.

114.   Tolverne Cottage was originally a tiny 'one up and one downer' and was occupied by Bessie Benarth, burnt at the nearby crossroads as a witch. Later much extended, it became the secret regional headquarters for American officers, and was visited by General Eisenhower shortly before the D-Day landings.

Institutions, Events and Happenings

115. *(opposite above)* American GIs in their PX club about 1943-4.

116. *(opposite below)* Victory celebrations, May 1945.

117. *(above)* The Bath and West Agricultural Show was periodically held at Truro during the 19th century, as seen here in 1861. It was heralded by a procession through the streets bringing livestock from the station.

118. Henry Williams acquired considerable wealth from the wool trade in the early 17th century, and endowed these Pydar Street almshouses for 'ten aged poor' in 1620, together with adjacent grazing lands, which later became the site of the workhouse and prison. The almshouse residents are seen here about 1900. Jerman Griest similarly endowed almshouses, which were later demolished to make way for the Pydar Street railway bridge.

119. Here we see the Truro City Volunteer Fire Brigade parading outside the cathedral about 1900, when the west front was still under construction.

120. *(above)* In 1870 the Truro Borough Police Force consisted of Superintendent Woolcock (seated), Sergeant Roberts, and Constables Coad, Collet, Scown and Bettison. The first policemen in Truro had been appointed in 1838.

121. *(overleaf)* Superintendent Angel and the Borough Police Force, *c.* 1900.

122. A busy scene outside Truro railway station before Coronation Terrace was built, around the turn of the century.

123. When the circus came to town, the elephants were taken for a bath in the Mill Pool, to the delight of their unofficial audiences. Today this area is beyond recognition, and the row of cottages (Neptune Cottages) has been demolished.

124.   The Royal Cornwall Infirmary, 1903. In 1790, money was raised by public subscription for 'a Publick Infirmary for the Sick, Lame and Poor'. The patronage of the then Prince of Wales entitled it to be known as the 'Royal' Cornwall Infirmary.

125.   The Gill family, who had extensive Truro business interests, were great enthusiasts in the early days of motoring. However, Mr. A. W. Gill's uninsured vehicle became a total wreck on 24 June 1906 after a petrol leak onto the hot exhaust caused it to catch fire at Liskey Hill, Perranporth.

126. The Wesleyans founded Truro College, later known at Truro School, in 1882. It is seen here about 1910.

127. The old cattle market at Castle Hill, *c*. 1913.

128. Young Truronians posing in River Street about 1914, outside the building which later became the home of the Royal Institution of Cornwall.

129. Hancock's Great World's Fair comes to town, 1920. Sophie Hancock's roundabout was the star attraction: she was a formidable lady, well able to handle employees and customers alike.

130. Cadets from Truro Cathedral School waiting at the railway station about 1920, about to leave on a school camp.

131. This drawing, published by the *Graphic* magazine on 29 May 1880, shows the Prince of Wales (later King Edward VII) laying the foundation stone of the cathedral.

132. (*opposite above*) In 1903 the Benediction of the Nave took place and on this occasion the Prince and Princess of Wales (later King George V and Queen Mary) travelled by special train from Paddington to Grampound Road Station. Here St Stephen's brass band provided a musical welcome, and the royal couple were greeted by Lord Falmouth (seen entering their carriage), and the High Sheriff of Cornwall.

133. (*opposite below*) The Benediction of the Nave ceremony took place on 15 July 1903. The royal carriage left in procession from Tregothnan, and is here seen proceeding down Richmond Hill.

134. *(above)* There was a civic procession from the Town Hall to the cathedral, where the dignitaries were awaited by the Bishop of Truro and the Archbishop of Canterbury. A congregation of 300, including 27 bishops, attended the service, and afterwards there was a civic banquet for 500 guests.

135. *(below)* Here the Bishop of Truro and his procession enter the west door for the Benediction of the Nave.

136. *(opposite above)* Boscawen Street was splendidly decorated for the Coronation celebrations of 1911, and the Truronians themselves are all in their best clothes.

137. *(opposite below)* The Royal Institution of Cornwall's new premises in River Street were opened by the Prince of Wales (later Edward VIII and then the Duke of Windsor) in 1919. Originally reserved for the privileged few, its doors are now open to the public free of charge.

Leisure Time

138. *(above)* This octagonal building was once a cock pit. It had a red-draped interior fringed with yellow, and gentlemen sat behind the cock pit barrier, while tradesmen sat in the gallery.

139. *(opposite above)* Boys intent on a game of marbles at Calenick, around the turn of the century. The old smelting house with its distinctive clock-tower can be seen in the background.

140. *(opposite below)* Fair on The Green, *c*. 1910, as the 'Gallopers' magnificent roundabout swings into action. In the 1920s the fair extended onto the quays, Quay Street, High Cross and the Moorfields, with competition for prestigious sites.

141. Visitors to Truro Fair
in 1905 anticipating the
delights of Hancock's Bio-
scope, the first moving
picture show. The great
Gavioli organ is on the left.

142. *(above)* Local folk ice-skating on Tresemple Pool, St Clement, in the early part of 1917.

143. *(right)* In the 1920s and 1930s, charabanc trips were very popular.

144. *(below)* William, Claude and Donald Gunn entered the Two Oars Two Paddles event at Hayle Regatta against their father's wishes, for he did not consider them ready to face the opposition from Hayle, Padstow and Newquay. However, when they won, their father was more than ready to forgive their disobedience!

People

145. *(above)* William Pasco, carpenter and founder of Pasco and Son of St Just, pauses with corking mallet in hand (1870).

146. *(overleaf)* The workmen who had constructed the choir of the cathedral gathered together, 1883.

148. John Equaggo Cockle's life-story sounds like a novel: James Equaggo of Ghana was befriended by a visiting ship-master, fell asleep on board, and found himself at sea! He was given the name 'John Cockle' as someone of that name listed in the ship's register was no longer aboard. He later married and settled at Chapel Hill, Truro.

149. Captain Peter Mortensen, known as 'Peter the Viking' or 'Mad Pete' was master and part-owner of the *Mary Barrow*. Born in Denmark, he was a familiar character of this area. He later operated a pleasure boat out of St Mawes.

147. (*overleaf*) Carvedras workers posing with tin ingots in 1892, shortly before the smelting works closed down. The bearded man on the right is James Symons, and the boy kneeling is John Penrose, who later went to America.

150. Donald Gunn of Malpas was a respected sportsman and won many trophies throughout Cornwall, including the Pair of Paddles sculling cup and the Whaler Race shield, both seen here. He was a boatman, oyster-dredger and oil worker, and built boats in his greenhouse.

151. John Cockle (son of no. 148 opposite), is a great Truro character and a familiar figure locally.

152. Dedication of the cathedral's bells, 1910. Here we see the bellringers on 21 June. The cathedral's architect, Frank L. Pearson, is in the back row (seventh from left); the bellfounder J. W. Taylor is in the front row (sixth from left); and a great benefactor of the cathedral, J. C. Daubuz, is also in the front row, on Taylor's right.